A.G.C.R.S.

Stanislaus à JESV MARIA Papczyński
1631–1701

To His Holiness, John Paul II,
a great Pole and a man of God
who is consecrated to Our Lady.

– *The Marians of the*
Immaculate Conception
of St. Stanislaus Kostka Province

Founder of the Marians

Founder of the Marians
Father Stanislaus Papczyński

Rev. Tadeusz Rogalewski, MIC

PRO CHRISTO ET ECCLESIA

Marians of the Immaculate Conception
Stockbridge, Massachusetts 01263
1997

Imprimi potest for English text
Very Rev. Walter M. Dziordz, MIC, Provincial
Stockbridge, MA, February 2, 1997

Translation and Editing from Polish into English:
Ewa St. Jean

Imprimi potest for original Polish text
Very Rev. Eugeniusz Delikat, MIC
Provincial
Warsaw, December 10, 1985

With the permission of the Metropolitan Curia in Warsaw
August 6, 1985
No. 5191 K 85

Library of Congress Catalog Card Number 96-08194
ISBN 0-944203-28-0
Copyright © 1997 Marians of the Immaculate Conception
All rights reserved.

Project coordinator and art selection :
Br. Andrew R. Mączyński, MIC
Designer for covers and photography insert: *Bill Sosa*
Editing: *Dave Came* and *Tim Flynn*
Typesetting: *Barbara York-Condron* and *Pat Menatti*

Front Cover: Close up of stone sculpture of the Venerable Servant of God, Fr. Stanislaus of Jesus Mary Papczyński — the Founder of the Marians of the Immaculate Conception. It stands in front of the little Church of the Cenacle in Góra Kalwaria, Poland, the site of Father Founder's burial.

Printed in the United States of America by the Marian Press, Stockbridge, Massachusetts 01263

TABLE OF CONTENTS

INTRODUCTION

For My thoughts are not your thoughts,
nor are your ways, My ways, says the Lord.
(Is 55:8)

This passage from Sacred Scripture is like a beacon that sheds light on how Our Merciful Lord guided Father Stanislaus of Jesus Mary Papczyński, the Founder of the Marians of the Immaculate Conception, on his journey through life. We will see in these pages how Father Founder surrendered his own will to that of God's, even though the way was fraught with numerous difficulties and setbacks that cost him dearly.

This is a particularly appropriate time to reflect on the heroic virtues and holy life of Father Stanislaus. Just last year, on May 18, 1996, we celebrated the 365th anniversary of his birth. And, on June 13, 1992, the Holy See recognized the heroic virtues of the Servant of God Stanislaus, declaring him "Venerable." A miracle obtained through the intercession of the Venerable Servant of God and recognized as such by the Holy See, is now the only thing necessary for his beatification.

From a purely human point of view, Father Stanislaus faced so many disappointments and so much adversity – including spiritual, mental, and physical sufferings – that one might conclude they were far beyond his endurance and strength. But just when it seemed that nothing else could be done in situation after situation, the Venerable Servant of God would entrust himself to God through Mary Immaculate's intercession and would then experience the Merciful Lord's miraculous intervention.

Because of this heroic surrender to the divine will and God's merciful response, Father Stanislaus's life is a rare and inspiring testimony of the wonderful dialogue between God and man. Time and again, this man of God turns to the Lord with childlike trust, and the Lord condescends to touch him with mercy and love. Even in his darkest moments, Father Stanislaus trusts that the Lord will not disappoint him.

Father Stanislaus of Jesus Mary Papczyński was the son of a blacksmith from the vicinity of Nowy Sacz, a city in southern Poland. After finishing his studies in the local grammar school, he decided to continue his education in the Jesuit college of Lwow (presently one of the largest Ukrainian cities) and then in the Piarist Seminary of Podolinec (now found in Slovakia).

After his ordination, Father Stanislaus became a professor and an educator of youth. Soon he became known as a preacher and spiritual director due to his zeal and devotion. In fact, we find inspiring references to the Servant of God as "an ardent apostle," "the advocate of the Poor Souls in Purgatory," a father of the poor, and the people's missionary. All of these titles attest to his rare apostolic fervor, profound faith, and brotherly love.

In all of his apostolic works and writings, Father Stanislaus emphasized the primacy of the Gospel commandment of loving God and your neighbor as the measure of true Christian maturity:

Above all, always love your neighbor with an unceasing love. Let nobody who does not love his neighbor think that he possesses true love. The love is true only when one loves his friends in God and his enemies for God's sake. (Orator Crucifix)

Father Stanislaus was known in particular as a fervent devotee of Mary Immaculate, to whom he consecrated his life and his apostolic works. He zealously spread her glory and sought to defend the truth of her Immaculate Conception through his writings and preaching, and most especially by founding the Marian Order in 1673. Entrusting himself entirely to Divine Providence and Our Lady's intercession, he established three main ideals or charisms for his followers: devotion to the Immaculate Conception; prayer for the dead; and assistance to pastors, especially in educating people in the truths of the faith.

The Venerable Servant of God's heroic virtues and holiness of life have been confirmed by numerous favors that God has bestowed upon the faithful who have sought his intercession. In fact, one might say that the Father Founder of the Marians of the Immaculate Conception continues his mission on our behalf in the courts of Heaven itself.

May this short biography enable us to see more clearly how the depths of God's love and mercy permeated the Venerable Servant of God's life. May it help bring each of us and other North American readers into closer contact with this inspiring personality. May it motivate each of us to a deeper study of Father Stanislaus's apostolic works and holy life. And may it inspire each of us to a truly heroic realization of our own vocation – regardless of the obstacles we face.

As we read this biography, let us observe closely how Father Stanislaus handles his many struggles and difficulties. Even more than this, let us learn from both his successes and failures, his strengths and weaknesses, of the call to be both fully human and fully God's. Let us find in Father Stanislaus's heroic story the truth of how the Lord God does not spare from suffering those who entrust themselves to Him. Rather, He uses that very suffering to purify the hearts of His chosen ones, so they can be transformed into the image of His Son.

May the Venerable Servant of God, Father Stanislaus of Jesus Mary Papczyński become for us an inspiring example of the call to love the Lord God and our neighbor. May we confidently address this saintly intercessor with these words of hope:

Venerable Father Stanislaus, to you we lift up our minds and hearts. We entreat you to listen to us with kindness, and show us the way through the dusk to the light.

Br. Andrew R. Mączyński, MIC
Vice-Postulator for North America
for the Canonization Cause
of the Venerable Servant of God
Stanislaus of Jesus Mary Papczyński

1. CHILDHOOD

Podegrodzie is an ancient village located in the heart of the Sandetian Valley, near Stary Sącz, on the left bank of the river Dunajec. There one can hear the eternal roar of the mountain river rolling its turbulent waters after freeing itself from the rocky arms of the Pieniny mountains. This picturesque region is criss-crossed with brooks which create many deep ravines and gorges. The sides of the Beskidy Mountains, which can be seen on the horizon, are covered with a green carpet of forest. Some mountaineers' cottages are scattered at the foot of the precipitous hills. All this creates an oasis of silence, quiet, and beauty.

In this charming corner of the Sandetian district, Stanislaus Papczyński was born early in the morning on Sunday, May 18, 1631. He was baptized on the same day at the local parish church and given the name Jan (John); he will change it to Stanislaus of Jesus and Mary later when he enters the religious life.

John's parents – Thomas and Sophia (nee Tacikowska) – were rather well-to-do people; they had two houses and a piece of land in Nowy Sącz. Thomas was a craftsman – a very able blacksmith. When he moved to Podegrodzie he was elected mayor of the village. In addition to this he was the administrator of the parish property. Sophia was most likely Thomas' third wife and apart from John gave him six daughters and one more son.

Both John's parents were very pious and raised their son in a deeply religious atmosphere. John's mother was particularly endowed with the virtue of patience and devo-

tion to the Most Blessed Virgin Mary. She eagerly partici-
pated in the parish activities; she belonged to the rosary
sodality of St. Anne and St. Francis.

John Papczyński developed a love for piety quite early.
This manifested itself not only in his prayer, in decorating
the pictures and wayside shrines, but also in pious child's
play. Under the influence of his mother, he developed a
devotion to the Most Blessed Virgin Mary; he venerated
her deeply, commended himself to her care every day –
and was not let down. Many times Mary would save him
from the dangers threatening his health and life.

One of the greatest graces which he received in childhood was the awakening of his mental abilities which
enabled this at first quite dull boy to begin school. He tried
to study, at first without any success, so he returned to
watching his father's sheep. When he tried for the second
time, a sudden change took place: a so far totally unintelli-
gent student learned the entire alphabet within one after-
noon. It is simply difficult to believe that the same John
Papczyński would later become an exemplary pupil, college student, brilliant speaker, famous lecturer, and writer.

Due to these changes he easily completed a three-grade
parish elementary school and then the first two grades of
grammar school.

2. DIFFICULT YOUTH

In May, 1646, young Papczyński set out to the town of
Jarosław, about 170 kilometers away, to continue his studies. He wanted to enroll in the third grade of the Jesuit

College. His cousin accompanied him on this journey. After ten weeks of studies, the two young men left Jarosław and went to Lwów to study at the Jesuit College there. But here a great disappointment waited for John: insufficiently prepared and lacking the necessary credentials, he was refused admission to the college.

In spite of this he did not give up the idea of studying at the college. He decided to supplement his education on his own and earned his living by giving lessons.

A year and a half later, in the summer of 1648, he became afflicted with a very serious disease. In those days a strange infectious disease raged in the vicinity of Lwów. It did not spare John. For almost four months he lay seized by high fever and his body was covered with annoying scales and sores. Seeing his poor health condition, his landlords asked him to leave. From that moment he roamed the streets all winter and, having no means to support himself, begged for alms. He was like Lazarus in his humiliation, but God's Providence was with him.

In February, 1649, John was miraculously healed: the scales and sores disappeared without any trace. At about the same time some of his neighbors, who came to Lwów to buy fish for the upcoming Lent, managed to locate him. They gave him some money from his parents. Since John was still very weak from his illness, his father sent a horse and a wagon to bring him home. After a month under his mother's tender care, John fully recuperated.

Having regained his health, Papczyński decided to continue his studies at the high school level. He needed to complete one more course in grammar as well as poetics and rhetoric. Therefore, at the end of April or the beginning of May, despite a three-year break in his studies, he left for Podoliniec (about 30 kilometers away) and entered the Piarist college there. One year later he had completed a full course of grammar.

Just around that time an epidemic broke out and was approaching Podoliniec. The Piarist Fathers closed the school. Once again John went back to Podegrodzie and watched his father's sheep. When the epidemic was over he did not return to Podoliniec but, instead, in June, 1650 went to Lwów again. Now he was gladly accepted by the Jesuits. Within a year he completed poetics and began rhetoric at their college.

He could not continue his studies, however, because after the defeat of the Polish army in May of 1652, the Cossacks were approaching Lwów. He left this city and went to the Jesuit college in Rawa Mazowiecka. Here he completed rhetoric and then a two-year philosophy course. Now the 23-year-old John Papczyński was a mature, spiritually formed man.

After his return to Podegrodzei, he was held in high regard and liked by all due to his education and spiritual formation. He was a slim young man, with a swarthy complexion, high forehead, and deep, pensive eyes. His education was something quite exceptional in the rural community. But it was mostly his spiritual attributes that made him stand out. He was sincerely religious, with a deep love for mortification, learning, and prayer. He thought more and more seriously about an even more perfect life. He wanted to dedicate himself totally to God and

His Most Holy Mother. Therefore, when his family in Podegrodzie attempted to get him married to a rich young girl and find him a good position, Papczyński left his family nest in June of 1654 and went to Podoliniec to begin a religious life at the Piarist Fathers.

3. THE ROAD TO A RELIGIOUS VOCATION

Walking the steep mountain paths, Papczyński made his way to the other side of the Carpathians and reached Podoliniec in the region of Spisz. He had once spent a year studying here and perhaps it was at that time that he decided to follow the religious way of life in the Community of the Piarist Fathers.

Upon his arrival, John Papczyński was received into the novitiate on July 2, 1654. Vested with the habit of the Order, he received his new name: Stanislaus of Jesus and Mary. From the very beginning of the novitiate, Stanislaus surrendered himself to the atmosphere and requirements of a truly religious life. Under the direction of his master, Brother Stanislaus trained himself in the life of practicing religious virtues, piety, and prayer. Soon he distinguished himself among the other novices with his love for contemplation and self-denial.

The religious life in Podoliniec was very rigorous. The novices performed many tasks in the household: chopping and carrying wood, fetching water from the well, feeding the cattle, working in the kitchen, and the like. Stanislaus fulfilled all his duties and orders eagerly and with great dedication.

The first year of the novitiate went by very quickly.

Since Stanislaus showed good progress in the spiritual life, his superiors allowed him to continue his studies in the second year of the novitiate. Therefore, in July, 1655, he was moved to Warsaw to study theology. At the time the Piarists' house in the capital city was located at Długa Street, and the clerics attended lectures at the monastery of the Order of the Reformati at Senatorska Street.

In September the Swedes captured Warsaw and it was with great difficulty that the studies could be continued under their occupation. The invading army plundered the capital city, spreading terror and violence among its inhabitants. Even the churches and monasteries were not spared. The Protestant soldiers treated the clergy with particular hatred.

One day novice Stanislaus was walking down the street with a fellow student – Joseph Starcek. Suddenly, in the vicinity of the Dominicans' church, they came upon a Swedish soldier who at once drew his sword at the brothers. Joseph fled immediately, but Stanislaus fell to his knees and bared his neck hoping for a martyr's death. The soldier struck his neck thrice with great force, causing intense pain, which the novice felt long afterwards, but he sustained no wound.

At the beginning of May, the Polish-Lithuanian army began an attack to liberate Warsaw. Stanislaus had to interrupt his studies as Swedes, leaving the city, burned and destroyed everything they could. The Piarists' house at Długa Street was burned, too. In the first days of July Warsaw was liberated – even though only for a month. But this period was very important for Papczyński because it was just then that he completed his novitiate and was allowed to make his religious profession. The celebration took place on July 22, 1656, when Warsaw was threatened by the Swedes yet again. Soon after, in the last week of July, the newly professed received his Minor Orders and the Sub-diaconate.

When, after a three day battle under the city walls, the Polish army was defeated by the united Swedish and Brandenburg forces, Papczyński, on the order of his superiors, left the capital and went to Podoliniec, and then, towards the end of September, to the newly opened establishment of the Piarist Fathers in Rzeszów.

But he did not stay there long, either. When the city was threatened by the army of Prince Rakoczy, another ally of the Swedes, Stanislaus returned to Podoliniec in March of 1657. He devoted all his spare time to studies and preparing for his lectures. The next year he was already teaching rhetoric – according to a textbook which he had written himself – at the Piarist College in Podoliniec, and in 1660 he began to teach the same course in their college in Rzeszów. Within the next few years he prepared and, in 1663, published his textbook under the title *Prodomus Reginae Artium* (Forerunner of the Queen of the Arts). Three more editions appeared by the year 1670.

4. THE PATH TO PRIESTHOOD

While he eagerly devoted himself to teaching rhetoric, subdeacon Papczyński was also preparing himself to enter the path of priestly life. A year after he began teaching at the college in Rzeszów, he was raised to the diaconate and soon after, on March 12, 1661, ordained priest by the Bishop of Przemśl, Stanislaus Sarnowski.

Now the scope of Father Stanislaus' duties was much broader as he had to combine his work as a teacher with his duties as a priest. Even when he was still only a lecturer, he tried to choose exercises and examples for his classes in such a way that they would not only help to mold character, but also form the students into good Catholics and Poles. But it was only now that he could work effectively as a shepherd of the souls.

Almost immediately he became known as an eager confessor and outstanding preacher. One of his first sermons, titled "In praise of the Mother of God", which he delivered in Rzeszów to the Marian sodality, has survived to our times. The sermon is a good example not only of this kind of literary work in the 17th century, but also an example of the depth of his approach from the theological point of view.

Papczyński demonstrated the fullness of his oratorical skills in Warsaw, where he was transferred in 1663. He was famous for his sermons preached in the churches of various religious orders. Particularly memorable were those in honor of St. Thomas which he delivered at the church of the Dominican Fathers. One of them titled "Doctor Angelicus" ("The Angelic Doctor"), printed and published in 1664, has been preserved to this day.

At the time Father Papczyński was a renowned confessor and spiritual director. Many entrusted him with the secrets of their conscience — prelates, bishops, senators and among the latter – the future King of Poland, John III Sobieski. One of his regular penitents from 1664 to 1667 was Anthony Pignatelli, the Apostolic Nuncio to Poland, and later Pope Innocent XII.

During this period Father Papczyński was also the Moderator of the Confraternity of Our Lady of Grace at the church of his (Piarist) order in Warsaw. In 1651, her picture in the Piarist church was crowned with the authorization of the Holy See. This was the first such crowning in Poland, and, in 1664, Our Lady of Grace was announced Patroness of Warsaw.

Father Stanislaus skillfully combined his pastoral activities with scientific work. In both fields he tried to use his talents and abilities fully; all this was supported and enhanced by his deep spirituality and mature interior life. It would seem that such a talented member of the Order should be accepted by everyone. Alas, this was not the case. It was during this period that a sharp conflict began to develop between Father Papczyński and some of his confreres. Later this conflict resulted in Father Stanislaus' leaving the Order.

5. A THORNY PATH

In order to understand Father Papczyński's later course of life, we need to go back in time a little and look at the beginnings of the Piarist Order in Poland. This order, founded by St. Joseph Calasantius in 1579, became quickly popular in Italy and the neighboring countries on its northern border. It came to Moravia as well, and from here, due to the events connected with the 30-year war, to Poland. King Ladislaus IV invited the Piarist Fathers to Warsaw in 1642. Prince Stanislaus Lubomirski invited them to Podoliniec, where they opened a novitiate and, in 1643, a college.

The time of Papczyński's studies in Podoliniec (1649-1650) was a time of crisis in the Congregation of the Piarist Fathers. The crisis lasted from 1646 to 1656. Pope Innocent X revoked their right to accept new candidates and take vows, putting all Piarists under the jurisdiction of local bishops. In spite of this, in 1648, the Piarists began to accept candidates under the name aggregati; they did the same in Podoliniec in 1650.

This may explain why Papczyński did not join their community immediately after he finished grammar school. He was probably waiting for the legal status of the Order to become clear. When in 1653 the Piarists were given permission to take religious vows, Papczyński could finally make a decision to enter their Order, which he did in 1654, after he had completed a philosophy course.

The next important legal act for the Piarist Order was a breve "Dudum felicis recordationis" issued by Pope Alexander VII on January 24, 1656, which restored their status as a religious order although, for the time being only with simple vows. It was in this same year that Papczyński completed the novitiate, and on July 22 made his profession. He was the first Pole to take vows in the renovated Congregation of the Piarist Fathers.

At first the foundations of the Piarists in Poland were under the administration of the Polish-German province with its main seat in Nikolsburg in Moravia. In 1662 the Polish province of the Piarist Fathers was established. In August, 1664, Papczyński was a delegate of the Warsaw house at the provincial chapter in Podoliniec, where he made a proposal regarding the right to elect their provincial superior and other superiors during such a chapter. So far, such an election was made by the general of the Order and his council in Rome.

Papczyński's proposal was accepted and the petition was sent. The general of the Piarists gave his answer in this matter to the Polish delegates during the general chapter in Rome in 1665. From then on the Polish province was to nominate three candidates, from which the general council would elect the provincial superior.

In the existing legal situation, some ethnic conflicts began to erupt, turning later into sharp clashes and antagonisms. These conflicts deepened when Papczyński began to oppose the suggestions to mitigate the Piarist rule. He wanted the Piarists to remain faithful to the ideal of poverty and religious observance.

He was accused of making trouble before Superior General, Father Cosmas Chiara, who, in turn, summoned him to Rome. Supplied with letters of recommendation from people faithfully testifying to his religious and pastoral zeal, he started on a strenuous and dangerous journey to the Eternal City towards the end of October, 1667. Before he left, he had made a moving statement titled "Protestatio Romam abeuntis" (Statement Upon Departing for Rome) in which he expressed his great humility, reverence, and obedience to his superiors.

The saintly General of the Piarists received Father Stanislaus very cordially and soon became convinced of his innocence. But his accusers did not give up and, during the chapter in Podoliniec, demanded, that he should be punished for being a "firebrand" and the destroyer of the peace in the province. When Father Chiara received the report from this provincial chapter, he found himself in a difficult position. He did intend to send Papczyński back to Poland, but now he changed his plan and ordered him to go to Nikolsburg in Moravia, the seat of the German province, towards the end of January, 1668.

However, Father Stanislaus did not stay there very long. With the permission of the German provincial, he went to Warsaw, in May of the same year.

6. AT THE CROSSROADS

After Father Stanislaus had returned to Poland, a new stage on his thorny path of life began. He faced new accusations and persecution from some members of the Congregation who were of a different nationality. But the Polish confreres from the Warsaw house came to his defense. The matter became increasingly more public and finally reached the Papal Nuncio, Cardinal Marescotti who demanded an explanation.

Following this, Father Opatowski, the Provincial Superior of the Piarists, conducted an investigation and on July 20, 1669, prepared a statement signed by him and his two assistants. In this document he declared that Father Papczyński's behavior was not that of a "firebrand" but

ther, due to a kind of zeal, and thus confirmed the innocence of the accused. But this did not help much.

In his concern for the peace in the province, Papczyński
decided to leave the Congregation. Therefore, in August,
1669, he sent a request to the Superior General asking to
be released from the vows and from the oath of perseverance in the Piarist Congregation.

Meanwhile an important legal act was issued — one of
great consequence for the future of the Congregation.
Pope Clement IX, in his breve "Ex iniuncto nobis" of
October 23, 1669, restored to the Piarists their previous
rights and privileges, and raised their congregation to the
rank of an order with solemn vows. After this act, each
member was obliged to take the vows again, if he wanted
to remain in the community.

Father Papczyński decided to take the arising opportunity to leave the Congregation. On December 20, 1669, he
sent a new request to Rome to be released from his obliga-
tions expressed in the simple vows he had taken. Assured
by experts on church law, that having taken only simple
vows, he was no longer subordinate to the Piarist superiors, he placed himself under the jurisdiction of the Bishop
Ordinary Andrew Trzebicki (+ 1679), the more so that he
was remaining on the territory of the Bishop's diocese
since September, 1669, as he lived at the Piarist residence
Kazimierz, near Cracow.

The fact that Papczyński sought the protection of the
Bishop exposed him to new persecutions by the Piarists.
On January 8, 1670, at the order of Provincial Opatowski,
he was forcibly removed from Kazimierz and sent first to

Podoliniec, and then to Prievidza in Hungary, where I was kept in the monastery prison for almost three months.

He was released only on March 22, at the intervention of the Bishop Auxiliary of Cracow Nicholas Oborski, and on April 2 returned to Kazimierz. On June 7, 167? according to the instructions he received from Rome Papczyński sent a letter with yet another request to released from the vows, but this time not to the Superi General, but to the Holy See. Besides, other Piarists were sending similar letters, too.

Pope Clement X in his breve "Cum felicis recordation is" of October 18, 1670 authorized the Superior General the Piarists to release from vows those members who had already submitted their requests in this regard. Father Chiara, in turn, in his letter to the Bishop of Cracow, date October 24, 1670, released Stanislaus Papczyński from his religious vows. The solemn act of secularization took place on December 11, 1670, and was performed by the Vice-Provincial of the Piarists, Father Michael Kraus.

Papczyński will confess later that, just before the cere mony of the dispensation from the vows and the oath perseverance in the Piarist Congregation, God inspired him to make new vows of chastity, obedience, and reli gious poverty. By then he had been contemplating for quite some time the founding of the Society of the Marian Fathers of the Immaculate Conception. During this cere mony Father Stanislaus made a new oblation for this new stage of his service to God and the Blessed Virgin Mary the religious life.

After the act of secularization, Stanislaus Papczyński

became a diocesan priest and fulfilled the duties of a chaplain to the Archconfraternity of the Immaculate Conception of the Blessed Virgin Mary, attached to the Church of St. James at Kazimierz, near Cracow.

7. THE BIRTH OF THE CONGREGATION OF MARIANS

Father Papczyński's act of oblation from December 11, 1670, is the first document confirming his intention to found the Congregation of Marians. This thought originated in his soul most likely during the time of his imprisonment at Podoliniec and then Prievidza. Papczyński had plenty of time for reflection, and during the long lonely weeks might have indeed conceived of such an idea. At any rate, he himself was convinced that this plan came from God's special inspiration.

According to his own intention, Papczyński still wore his religious habit even though, at that point, he had passed to the ranks of the lay clergy. He would soon exchange the black habit, of the order of St. Joseph Calasantius, for the white one of the congregation which he was going to found. The white color was to symbolize the purity of the Immaculately Conceived Blessed Mother. The ceremony of investiture was to take place in 1670, before the end of the octave of the Immaculate Conception in the Bishop's palace. Alas, the ceremony was cancelled for unknown reasons.

Therefore, Papczyński still wore the Piarist habit, although the Piarists were very much against it. He wore this habit as a form of protest, since the Piarists refused to give him a document to certify that he had been a member of their congregation. Not only did the superiors not want to give him such a certificate, they even summoned him before the Bishop's tribunal and later made an appeal to the Apostolic Nuncio, Angel Ranuzzi.

In December, 1670, the Servant of God had to face a painful disappointment when Bishop Oborski refused to support him in founding the new congregation. This caused a serious internal crisis in Papczyński. He was besieged by doubts as to whether his decision to leave the Piarists was right. He was even going to return to them and to this end he submitted a request to be read-mitted. This attempt to return to the Congregation was a kind of test he set for himself. He wanted to determine whether God wanted him to spread the devotion to the Immaculate Conception and follow the ideal of poverty at the Piarists — or in a new order. The Piarists, gathered at their general chapter in Rome in May, 1671, refused Father Stanislaus's request.

Now Papczyński had no doubts regarding his plans for the future. He decided to adhere to them, even though he was being offered various posts in the church. The Bishop of Płock, John Gębicki wanted to call him to be his con-fessor and offered him the canonicate at the Płock cathe-dral. The Bishop of Cracow, Andrew Trzebicki also offered him church honors and benefices, and many reli-gious orders invited him to join them. But he rejected all such offers seized by this one great thought — that of founding an order in honor of the Immaculately

Conceived Blessed Mother. Since he saw no possibility of realizing his plan in the diocese of Cracow, he moved to Mazovia in the summer of 1671 and placed himself under the care of the Bishop of Poznań, Stephen Wierzbowski (1667-1687), who promised him his assistance. At the beginning of September 1671, following the advice of his confessors, he went to live at the court of a nobleman, James Karski, in Lubocz, near Nowe Miasto on the Pilica river, also located in the diocese of Poznań. He fulfilled the duties of a chaplain there.

Soon, with Bishop Wierzbowski's permission and with the knowledge of the Apostolic Nuncio, during the octave of the Feast of the Nativity of the Most Holy Virgin Mary, Father Stanislaus was vested in the new habit, similar to the one he wore at the Piarists, different only in color. A very solemn ceremony of investiture took place before the altar, in which the picture of the Immaculate Conception of Our Blessed Mother was venerated. The picture, a gift from Pope Urban VIII, was brought by the Karski family from Rome. Later the picture was placed in the church of the Congregation at Marian Forest (Puszcza Mariańska) and became famous for many graces. Everyone present at the ceremony realized how important this event was. This was the moment when the first seed of a new religious family — the first male clerical order on Polish territory — was sown and began to take root.

8. FOR THE GLORY OF MARY IMMACULATE

The guiding principle followed by Father Papczyńsk as he was founding the Congregation of Marians was t spread the cult of the Immaculate Conception of the Mos Holy Virgin Mary. From the very beginning, this ide became simultaneously the principal goal of th Congregation. It found expression in the very name of th institute, the founding of which Papczyński declared in hi solemn act of oblation of December 11, 1670. It was sup posed to be an institute "of the Immaculate Conception."

At that time, Father Stanislaus dedicated himself to Mar the Virgin Mother of God "conceived without sin" s deeply that he vowed to defend her honor — the conse quence of the unique privilege of the Immaculat Conception — even at the cost of his life. It was the so called "Vow of Blood" taken by the "immaculists" in vari ous countries of Europe since about 1615. Fathe Papczyński followed their example.

The truth about the Immaculate Conception of th Most Holy Virgin Mary was not obvious to all the faithfu of that time . Its dogmatic formulation was to take plac only in 1854, even though this truth had been proclaime in the regular teaching of the Church long before. Th Popes of the 17th century — Paul V, Gregory IV, an Alexander VII also confirmed this truth. But the contro versies and disputes between the "macculists" an "immaculists" still existed. Our founder was a representa tive of the latter group.

His views on the subject were expressed in a poe

published in 1663 in "Prodomus Reginae Artium," which contained an interesting attempt to prove the privilege of the Immaculate Conception "ex consequentibus," that is, from the absence of those consequences attributed to Original Sin in the life of the Blessed Virgin Mary, thereby proving that she was never stained by it, and so was indeed Immaculately Conceived.

His other poem "Triumphus" was dedicated to the same mystery. It was printed in a book by D.C. Kochanowski titled "Novus Asserendae Immaculatae Conceptionis Deiparae Virginis Modus." The book was published in 1669, and according to Papczyński, contained a new convincing proof of the Immaculate Conception.

He also discussed this truth in his sermons written at the time of his affiliation with the Piarists, the sermons "on the exceptional and free from the original stain Conception of the Blessed Virgin Mary." He preached these sermons and had them published, but they did not survive to our times.

Papczyński combined his efforts at founding the Congregation of Marians with his pastoral duties at the home of the Karski family. He introduced among the members of the household the practice of singing the Rosary in common. This custom survived there for many years. It was remembered even a hundred years later.

Father Stanislaus devoted a lot of his time to contemplation. Its fruit were the two books which he wrote in Lubocz: "Templum Dei Mysticum" (The Mystical Temple of God) and "Norma Vitae" (The Rule of Life). The first one is a textbook on asceticism, one of the first in the

Church and intended chiefly for the laity. The other one is on the religious rule for the future Marians.

9. MARTYR'S ROAD

Time was passing, but Father Stanislaus still did not have suitable candidates for the Congregation. There were a few who expressed interest but were not accepted as they did not possess the qualities required for the religious life. Moreover, Father Stanislaus still did not have a suitable place where the newly accepted candidates could live.

To make matters worse, what had already happened once in Cracow repeated here in Mazovia. Just like Bishop Oborski, who was at first quite sympathetic to the whole idea, but later refused to support him, similarly now Bishop Wierzbowski, apparently cautioned by someone biased, began to express serious reservations about the erection of the Congregation of Marians in his diocese. He did not dash Father Stanislaus' hopes but made his acceptance contingent upon the permission of the Holy See.

Therefore, Father Papczyński began to make efforts to obtain the necessary permission from Rome. He submitted the matter to some plenipotentiary who was leaving for the Eternal City. However, the man did not treat the matter seriously and took no steps to pursue it. A year went by but things were at a standstill. All Father Stanislaus' efforts and expenses were wasted.

This was a very difficult period for the Servant of God also for one more reason. He had to face constant persecution by some ill-disposed people. They used gossip, slander, and derision; they wrote malicious libels to humiliate the future founder of the Congregation and to upset his efforts in this regard. They distorted the truth about his stay at the Piarists and the circumstances surrounding his leaving this order. It became necessary to respond to these attacks even if only for the sake of the future candidates to the Congregation who should know the true version of these events. It was with this purpose in mind that Father Papczyński wrote "Apology," in which he revealed the real reasons behind his decision to leave the Piarists.

It seems strange that Father Stanislaus experienced so many troubles in the realization of his plans. What was the cause of the hatred that he was faced with all the time? Father Papczyński knew that everything great is born in pain, so he did not give up and remained firm in his intentions.

He did have many friends who supported him and reaffirmed his conviction that his plans were a part of God's Providence. One of Father Stanislaus' most trusted friends was Father Francis Wilga, the Superior at the Camaldulese monastery at Królewska Góra near Warsaw (presently known as Bielany).

In the fall of 1672, Father Papczyński visited him to ask his advice. He had contacted this wise man many times before, but this time the matter was of utmost importance. Informed about the mounting difficulties, Father Wilga advised Papczyński to try and find a companion with whom he could begin a religious life. Only then should he seek the approval of the Holy See.

10. THE FIRST MARIAN MONASTERY

Following Father Wilga's advice, Father Papczyński turned his attention to a hermitage in the Korabiew Forest, about 40 kilometers away from Lubocz, where a certain war veteran, a 30-year-old Stanislaus Krajewski, lived with his companions. The man settled on a piece of land given to him by King Michael in 1670, and lived the life of a hermit there. It was most likely in the fall of 1672 that Father Papczyński went to see him and revealed to him his intention to found the first Marian monastery at his hermitage.

Krajewski gladly accepted the proposal, offered his estate to Father Stanislaus, declared himself ready to recognize him as his Superior and persuaded one of his companions to do the same. He also agreed to accept "The Rule of Life" presented by Father Stanislaus.

Later he urged Father Stanislaus many times to speed up the realization of his plans. But Father Stanislaus was very cautious and kept putting the final decision off. He was troubled by certain traits of Krajewski's character, which suggested that he was not a suitable candidate for the religious life. He loved his freedom too much, and this did not give promise that he would be able to bear the rigors of obedience well. Moreover, he was too ambitious, inconstant, stubborn and lacking in spiritual maturity.

Papczyński prayed to God for guidance and again asked his confessors and friends for advice. Since they all encouraged him to make the attempt, he finally decided nd invited Krajewski to Lubocz. There on July 4, 1673, 1e accepted his act of oblation to the Society of the mmaculate Conception and his oath of perseverance and ubmission to the Rule. Krajewski was vested with a vhite habit and received a religious name — John of the mmaculate Conception.

It was now necessary to inform the church authorities bout this event. For this reason, Father Papczyński went o the nunciature. The new Nuncio, who had recently rrived in Poland, gave his permission to celebrate Mass n the chapel which Krajewski had begun to build on the ite. Then Father Stanislaus contacted Bishop Wierzbowski and obtained his permission to make a nonth's retreat at the Korabiew hermitage.

The time to leave the hospitable house of the Karski amily had finally arrived. After two years of living nder the same roof, the hosts reluctantly said goodbye o their saintly chaplain and friend. On September 30, 673, Father Papczyński arrived at the Korabiew orest. Krajewski was not there, but the two remaining ompanions of the host welcomed him and helped him nto his new quarters. One of these men was Simon Werbicki, a Franciscan tertiary, who had returned from taly where he had lived as a hermit near Subiaco for our years. The other man was an organist. They also ad a boy servant.

Early in the morning on the next day, Father Papczyński woke the Korabiew hermits up for prayers ecause he wanted to initiate them into the religious dis- ipline from the very beginning. But he discovered very quickly that he was dealing with people who were not used to obedience and penance. The men, in turn, expressed their unhappiness with the new orders and complained when Krajewski returned to the hermitage the following day.

In this situation, Father Stanislaus decided to leave the hermitage after the month's retreat was over. He asked Krajewski to give him a piece of land on his property where a house of prayer could be built and where more suitable candidates could be gathered. Krajewski himself was to fulfill the duties of the procurator of the Congregation. After a few days of reflection, Krajewski accepted Father Stanislaus' proposal and, on October 7, 1673, drew up an act of donation.

11. THE CANONICAL VISITATION OF THE KORABIEW HERMITAGE

However, this time again, matters took a different course than Father Stanislaus had planned. A pastoral visitation of the parish in Jeruzal was taking place at the time. Since the Korabiew hermitage was located on the parish territory, Bishop Stanislaus Jack Święcicki, Vicar of Warsaw, was to visit it as well. This was what Father Stanislaus himself had recommended to Bishop Wierzbowski (Ordinary of the Poznań-Warsaw diocese). Supplied with the necessary instructions from the Ordinary, Bishop Święcicki arrived at the hermitage on October 24, 1673, and was to decide its future.

It was very likely that he would put a ban on it as many

ad things about it had reached the Bishop of Poznań. The lifestyle of the Korabiew hermits was too unrestrained, if not outright scandalous. This was why Father Stanislaus suggested the visitation in the first place. To make matters worse, Krajewski was away when the Visitator arrived. This made the Bishop furious.

He was about to remove the unruly hermits from the forest, but decided to give them another chance and put them to a test. From now on they were obliged to follow strictly "The Rule of Life" formulated by Father Papczyński. The Visitator added a few of his own statutes describing the spiritual exercises and penances appropriate for the hermits. There was, among others, a strict order to keep silence on certain days of the week, a requirement of self-flagellation in public, and a ban on owning money and leaving the monastery.

Father Stanislaus, who intended to leave the place after the retreat was over, was ordered to stay and was made superior of the "Marian hermits." The latter were to swear obedience to the Bishop of the diocese.

One might expect that the Korabiew hermits would not accept such rigorous measures and leave their hermitage. Indeed, they abandoned it immediately leaving only Father Stanislaus and Krajewski.

The visitation mentioned here was of fundamental importance to the Congregation which Father Papczyński was founding because the Bishop Visitator's act of October 24, 1673, is considered by the Marians today as the beginning of their religious family.

12. DIFFICULT BEGINNINGS FOR THE NEW CONGREGATION

The early stages of the new congregation, after the monastery at the Korabiew Forest was established, were very difficult. Father Stanislaus's only companion remaining after the canonical visitation opposed and ignored both "The Rule of Life" and the Bishop's statutes. Soon it became evident that he showed no promise as the future Marian. He fought the Father Founder ruthlessly, and towards the end of 1675, the relations between the two men became very bad.

One day Krajewski insulted Father Stanislaus, beat him severely, and ran away from the hermitage at night breaking the oath of perseverance which he had taken. Soon after, acting possibly as the Procurator of the Marians, he established (on the foundation received from Bishop Wierzbowski) an institute called "The Hermits of St. Onuphrius," at the Church of St. Martin in New Jerusalem (presently known as Góra Kalwaria).

Since he was still collecting donations for the "Marian hermits" in the vicinity of the Korabiew foundation and made claims to it, Father Papczyński took the matter to church tribunal. The trial took place on April 30, 1677, and as a result Krajewski relinquished his claims to both foundations — at the Korabiew Forest and New Jerusalem.

Later, with Bishop Święcicki's permission, he moved with his institute and settled on a new foundation in the village of Wygnanka, near Lutkowo, located two miles away from the Korabiew hermitage. After some time however, he returned to the Marians, took the vows and died as a member of this congregation before 1685.

From the very beginning the founder of the Marians experienced problems not only with the candidates to the Congregation but also with the statutes imposed upon the "Marian hermits" by Bishop Święcicki. It was never Father Papczyński's intention to found the Marians as a contemplative community which would be prevented from conducting any pastoral work outside the walls of the monastery. He intended his Society of Mary Immaculate to be apostolic in character. The rules left by the Visitator did not take these plans into account. But Father Papczyński submitted himself to the Bishop's statutes and tried to follow them for the sake of his own salvation.

The Servant of God Papczyński skillfully combined the work of the founder of a congregation with his pastoral service. With the Bishop's permission, he often left the monastery to aid pastors in the neighboring parishes. Only two weeks after the retreat, he went to the parish church in Chojnata where, at the Feast of St. Martin on November 11, 1673, he gave a homily during which he had a prophetic vision. He saw in ecstasy the victory of the Polish army led by Hetman Sobieski over the Turks at Chocim.

He shared this news with the many faithful gathered in the church. He proclaimed God's word not only from the pulpit, but taught catechism, heard confessions, and conducted devotions. He was most glad to do pastoral work among the simple people. He taught them to live according to Christ's teaching, prompted them to abandon sin, and encouraged them to practice Christian virtues.

Although his soul needed the apostolic work, he did not neglect his nascent Congregation. In order to give it the right profile, he constantly modified his "Rule of Life." The purpose of these changes was to make the congregation less eremitical and more apostolic after all. Thus, our Founder gradually moved away from the statutes imposed by Bishop Święcicki and, with the approval of the church authorities, realized his own concepts.

13. EFFORTS TO OBTAIN THE CHURCH'S APPROVAL

The legal status of the tiny religious community at the Korabiew Forest was still temporary. Therefore, Father Papczyński began efforts to obtain an erection decree to build a house of retreat. The matter took seven months and it was only on June 15, 1674, that he received such a decree. The document confirmed the permission which Bishop Święcicki had already given to build a chapel in honor of Our Lady's Immaculate Conception and St Michael the Archangel. Since Krajewski had started to build the chapel on ground that was too damp, Papczyński decided to move the construction to a higher place where the soil was more sandy. The new chapel was to be bigger than the one in the original plan.

One can imagine the enthusiasm with which Father Stanislaus set about raising the new buildings so needed by his community. The work on leveling the ground, clearing the forest, and preparing the wood for the building began

The Servant of God did the hard physical work and it is not known who, besides Krajewski, helped him with it.

We have no information about any other members of the Korabiew community from that period of time. People inspired and attracted by the renowned sanctity of the Servant of God began to visit his hermitage in ever increasing numbers. Perhaps some of them helped with the construction of the chapel, too.

It was also necessary to set up at least a small farm and a vegetable garden. This again required clearing the forest and tidying the place up. Later Father Stanislaus' spiritual sons reverently showed the novices the places sanctified by his toil.

The next stage, after receiving the permission to build the house of retreat, were the efforts, begun towards the end of 1674, to obtain the approval of the Holy See for the newly founded Congregation. Father Stanislaus addressed his petition to Pope Clement X who turned it over to the Sacred Congregation for the Bishops and Religious. The Congregation sent a copy of the petition to the Apostolic Nuncio in Poland, Francis Buonvisi, who, in turn, sent it to Bishop Wierzbowski. There is no information about the further course of the matter. It remained, most likely, at the chancellory of the Bishop of Poznań for the time being.

In 1676, Father Papczyński was undergoing another crisis of his Marian vocation. It was then that Krajewski left him and only Brother John of St. Mary remained, but, supposedly, left later as well. The crisis must have been serious indeed if in the summer of the same year Father Papczyński submitted a request to be accepted by the

Piarists again. The request was accepted by their provincial chapter in August of 1676, but rejected by the general chapter on May 18, 1677, citing the decisions of previous chapters which forbade accepting those who had once left the Congregation. However, before this answer came from Rome, a few candidates of great spiritual and intellectual attributes came to Father Stanislaus, towards the end of 1676. This helped him to overcome the crisis.

14. THE FIRST VOCATIONS

The information about Father Papczyński's first companions in the Marian vocation is very scant. The members of the Korabiew community left him immediately after the Bishop's visitation and only Krajewski remained a little longer. Later, even he gave up the religious life under the direction of Father Stanislaus and tried to establish his own institute. Yet, after some time, he returned to the Korabiew Forest, submitted himself to the direction of the founder of the Marians, entrusted him with the execution of his will and died piously as a member of the Congregation.

Apart from Krajewski, these names are mentioned as Father Stanislaus's first subordinates: Father Stanislaus of St. Ann, Father Joseph of All Saints, Father Cyprian of St Stanislaus, Father Constantine of St. Michael, Father Peter, and Brother Anthony Cieński. Father Joseph of All Saints — the first priest ordained in the Congregation, and Brother Anthony Cieński distinguished themselves from this group with the holiness of their lives.

Father Papczyński took great care of his first candidates

as he initiated them into the religious life. He personally supervised the studies of those confreres who were preparing for the priesthood. In his formation work, he strongly emphasized obedience, knowing very well how important this virtue is in organizing a religious community.

Seeing the devastation which the habit of drinking alcohol brought upon the Polish nation, he obligated the Marians to total abstinence from alcoholic beverages, and in his sermons propagated the idea of sobriety among the people. The ban on using spirits, wine, and mead can be found already in the Visitation Act of 1673.

Later, the Servant of God would often refer to this ban and encourage his confreres to remain sober and thus to honor Christ's thirst on the Cross. Those who would not observe the ban risked losing God's blessing. In his will, Father Papczyński wrote that spirits were forbidden to all the confreres "because this beverage is foreign to our Congregation for God's mysterious mercy."

Soon the Korabiew hermitage became famous in the area as Father Stanislaus' saintliness attracted many pious people. Some even desired to stay by his side and establish closer ties with him. Sophia Potkańska and her daughter were among such zealous souls. Mrs. Potkańska's husband decided to join the Order of the Reformati, and she herself intended to found a nunnery of the Sisters of the Immaculate Conception. She wanted to do it with Father Stanislaus' assistance and on the grounds near his hermitage. Father Stanislaus declined the offer. Perhaps he did not see in the two ladies sufficient signs of vocation to undertake such an effort. Or perhaps he did not want to expose the new Congregation to such difficulties as those that his own work had to encounter. To spare them such an ordeal, he persuaded Sophia Potkańska to fund a nunnery for the Dominican Sisters in New Jerusalem.

During the first stage of his stay at Korabiew, Father Stanislaus published "Templum Dei Mysticum" (The Mystical Temple of God) — an ascetic piece which he had prepared much earlier. The work was printed in Cracow in 1675. The author presents in it a human soul as the temple of God. Using various allegories, he discusses man's spiritual faculties and the means helping man to attain Christian perfection.

Watching the growth of his religious community, Father Stanislaus decided to secure its legal status. To this end he began efforts to obtain the approval for the Congregation from the Polish Parliament (Seym). He had to visit many lay and church offices in order to secure the possessions of his institute and obtain the necessary privileges. As a result of his endeavors he received the approval of the Parliament on April 27, 1677, which confirmed the rights of the Congregation to the grounds on which stood the monastery buildings as well as to a meadow nearby. Now Father Papczyński could, if necessary, defend the rights of his community in the civil courts.

15. ASSISTING THE POOR SOULS
IN PURGATORY

Both the visitation document of 1673 and the Seym privilege of 1677 mention the fact that the Marians had a duty to help the souls in Purgatory. They were obliged to pray the entire Rosary and say the Office for the Dead every day. This duty will be emphasized even more strongly in later documents.

The idea of helping the souls suffering in Purgatory was the result of both the need of the times and Father Stanislaus' deep personal experiences. The never ending wars with Moscow, the Cossacks, Turks, Tartars, and Sweden, as well as the internal turmoil brought a rich harvest of death. Natural disasters, hunger, and epidemics increased it even more. People were dying by the thousands and so often going unprepared before God for their last judgement.

Christian love prompted Father Stanislaus to think about those prisoners of Purgatory and rush to their aid. It seemed to him that they were stretching their arms out to him and begging for help. In his long prayers, sometimes lasting the entire night, he would descend in spirit to Purgatory and stay with the souls suffering there.

A particular revival of the Servant of God's devotion to the souls in Purgatory took place in 1675, when he most probably served as a chaplain of the Polish army led by Hetman John Sobieski fighting with the Turks in the Ukraine. Father Stanislaus kept in his pastoral care the souls of the soldiers who died in battles and prayed on their graves. It is believed that the souls of many of the fallen soldiers appeared to him and asked his intercession before God. Under the influence of these experiences and after deep personal reflection, the Servant of God decided that helping the souls of the dead, especially those who perished during a war or pestilence, should be the second goal of his Congregation.

Tradition left us a few other accounts of Father Papczyński's experience of Purgatory. During one of his visits to Lubocz, at a family gathering where many lay and religious guests were present, when all made their way to the dining table after the service, Papczyński fell into an ecstasy in which, as he confessed later, he watched the suffering of the souls in Purgatory. When he came to himself, he left the dining hall and started on his way back to his monastery. To his confreres, surprised by such a quick return, he said: "Pray, brethren, for the souls in Purgatory, for they suffer unbearably." Then he locked himself in his cell for three days and prayed for the souls suffering in Purgatory.

It was most probably in 1693 that Father Papczyński made a pilgrimage to the miraculous picture of the Blessed Mother in Studzianna, about fifty kilometers away from the Korabiew Forest. Father John Ligęza, Father Papczyński's close friend and confessor, was the Superior at the Oratorian monastery in Studzianna at that time. After celebrating Mass before the miraculous picture Father Stanislaus went to his cell where he fell into a state of ecstasy during which he experienced the suffering of the departed souls. After a few hours, he regained awareness. Without taking any meal, he began his return journey to the Korabiew Forest. There, in silence and with great attention, he prayed and did penance for the dead.

His contemporaries recalled that the Servant of God frequently locked himself in his cell to pray and to visit in spirit the souls in Purgatory. He would communicate with these souls doing penance for their sins. The suffering souls asked him to continue coming to their aid through his Congregation. Many times during such ecstasies, he himself physically experienced the pains suffered by the souls in Purgatory. On such occasions, he would ask God to increase his suffering and diminish the punishment for the souls. In this same spirit, he formed his brothers in the religious life.

The life of this intercessor for the souls in Purgatory was full of sacrifice. To make himself even more pleasing to God, he would impose upon himself various penances: he often extended his prayers very late into the night, he kept strict fasts, scourged himself, did a lot of hard physical work, and made long journeys on foot. Added to this were constant persecutions by his enemies and various other adversities.

He prophesied to his confreres that many difficult times awaited them in the future. He called his monastery "Noah's Ark" or "Korab" from the name of the village Korabiewice. He encouraged his brethren to seek shelter from the troubles and come within this "ship" under the protection of Mary Immaculate. He prophesied that the waters of slander and persecution would surround this "vessel" just like the waters of the flood surrounded Noah's Ark. But they would eventually subside and the "Korab" would sail out upon calm waters. This hope found expression in the Seal of the Congregation, where, upon Father Stanislaus' orders, the image of a dove holding an olive branch in her beak, a symbol of final deliverance, was to be placed.

16. THE FOUNDATION OF THE MONASTERY IN NEW JERUSALEM

The holiness of the Servant of God continued to draw many people to the Korabiew Forest and attracted new vocations. Soon the number of the brothers grew to the point that it was possible to consider establishing a second religious house. A good opportunity soon presented itself, because Bishop Wierzbowski, the founder of New Jerusalem, was bringing various religious orders to this town, to ensure its pastoral care. In his search, he turned his attention to the Marians as well. Father Papczyński gladly responded to the Bishop's call and on April 30, 1677, the Congregation took over the Chapel of St. Martin in New Jerusalem, which had belonged to Krajewski before. Soon after, at Bishop Wierzbowski's wish, he himself moved to New Jerusalem.

New Jerusalem was built in the place where a village called Góra near Czersk had been located. In 1670, the Bishop of Poznań, Stephen Wierzbowski, obtained foundation privileges from the king and decided to turn it into a sanctuary modeled after Jerusalem in the Holy Land. For this purpose he built various churches and chapels which were at the same time the Stations of the Cross.

These churches and chapels were looked after by various religious communities. The Oratorians took care of the Church of the Holy Cross, the Piarists — the Church of the Birth of Our Lord Jesus, the Dominicans — the monastery on Mount Zion, the Dominican Sisters — the Church of the Last Supper.

In 1677, at the initiative of the Dominicans, certain changes were introduced in the administration of the churches in the town. The Dominicans took over the Chapel of St. Martin, changing its name to that of the Assumption of the Blessed Virgin Mary, the Dominican Sisters moved to Mount Zion, and the Marians took over the Church of the Last Supper.

The foundation document of November 22, 1677, giving the Marians the right of ownership to both this church and the adjacent fields and buildings, placed on them the duty of accompanying the pilgrims along their way to the Stations of the Cross. The pilgrims would gather at the Cenacle to ponder the mysteries of the Last Supper, the reminder of which was a table standing in the middle of the church. From here they would proceed to the particular Stations of the Cross.

The Church of the Last Supper was built in 1674. It had stone walls and a shingle roof with an ave-bell tower, a big main door, and a smaller side door leading to the monastery. The founder of the Cenacle left the Marians the surrounding grounds as well. They were swampy and not tillable.

Papczyński decided to drain them. He dug ponds that could be stocked with fish, drained the swamps, and turned the morass, which the foundation document called a "lake", into a meadow. He even managed to obtain a piece of tillable land. He did all this with a handful of his confrères, without any funds and among unfriendly neighbors.

It was these neighbors who, for some incomprehensible reasons, were hostile to the newcomers and disturbed their peace. They questioned the Marians' rights to the fields which they had obtained by draining the swamps. They would even raid the property causing a lot of damage. One such attack, which occurred on August 20, 1678, is mentioned in a report in the Warsaw consistory. During this incident, some of the inhabitants of the village of Chynów beat Father Stanislaus severely, hurled insults at the brothers, threatened to kill them, and caused a lot of damage in the woods. There were more such attacks.

17. THE APPROVAL OF THE CONGREGATION BY THE DIOCESAN AUTHORITIES

A year after the monastery in New Jerusalem was established, Father Papczyński resumed his efforts to obtain the approval of the church authorities for his Congregation. After his first attempt in 1674, the matter came to a standstill, so it became necessary to take a different course.

At the moment it was not possible to obtain the approbation of the Holy See on the basis of "The Rule of Life," because the decree of the Fourth Lateran Council of 1215 did not allow for the approval of religious institutes with rules different from those already in existence. For the time being, it would be necessary to obtain the approval of the Bishop Ordinary who had the authority to erect the institute of the hermits on the basis of the regulations of the general laws of the Church.

At Father Papczyński's request, Bishop Wierzbowsk

began in, 1678, the proceedings leading towards the approval of the Congregation of Marians in his diocese. The matter was considered at two subsequent trials: on June 17 and November 16 of that same year, and was concluded on April 21, 1679, with the erection of the Congregation on diocesan statutes.

Bishop Wierzbowski's erection document describes the Marians as hermits of the second degree, places them under the protection of the Bishop Ordinary, approves their own rules, and makes Father Papczyński the Superior of the Congregation for life. It also recalls one of the goals of the Congregation, that of aiding the souls in Purgatory, especially the souls of those who perished during a war, pestilence, or as a result of some other disaster, as well as the souls deprived of any help whatsoever.

Bishop Wierzbowski commends people sentenced to death to the special pastoral care of the Marians. He orders them to console the condemned, support them with prayer, and accompany them to the place of execution.

8. FRIEND OF THE VICTOR OF VIENNA

After obtaining the approval of the Bishop Ordinary, Father Papczyński procured also a privilege from King John III Sobieski. During his stay at New Jerusalem, on June 2, 1679, the King drew up a document in which he confirmed the privileges bestowed upon the Marians by his predecessors, added new ones, made a new grant of land, adding it to the property of the Congregation in the Korabiew Forest, took the Marians under his protection, guaranteed their peace and inviolability, and expressed a wish for this Congregation to spread to other parts of his kingdom.

John III Sobieski often visited Bishop Wierzbowski in New Jerusalem and on such occasions he would probably see Father Papczyński, too. According to tradition, these contacts were frequent and friendly. It was perhaps still during Father Stanislaus' stay in Warsaw that Sobieski listened to his sermons, asked his advice, and sought his spiritual guidance in the confessional. Later, as a king, he probably did the same in New Jerusalem.

One of the witnesses in the information process stated that he had read letters written by King Sobieski to Father Papczyński. Unfortunately, these letters are missing. On the other hand, the popular story about Father Stanislaus participation in the Battle of Vienna is probably based on the isolated and rather unreliable testimony of only one witness in the information process. This piece of information should be considered erroneous for it does not have any confirmation in the historical documents.

It is certain, however, that before he left for his Vienna campaign, John III Sobieski commended himself to Father Papczyński and his confreres' prayers, which is later mentioned by Father Wyszyński. These facts demonstrate that the generation contemporary to the Servant of God was convinced that the relations between him and the victor of Vienna were very close indeed.

19. ON THE ROAD TO PAPAL APPROBATION

The next significant legal act following the canonical

erection of the Congregation in 1679 and King Sobieski's privilege was the breve of Pope Innocent XI of March 20, 1681 "Cum sicut accepimus." This document bestowed many privileges upon the Marians, such as plenary indulgences granted upon entering the Congregation, at the hour of death, and on the Feast of the Immaculate Conception of the Blessed Virgin Mary. Various partial indulgences were also granted, e.g., for participation in the Holy Mass and other devotions, as well as for performing acts of mercy. It is not known how this breve was obtained. Perhaps Bishop Wierzbowski himself asked the Pope for it, when he informed him about the erection of the Congregation in his diocese.

The shepherd of Poznań was very anxious about the future of the Marians, so he kept encouraging them in their efforts to obtain the approbation of the Holy See. He himself took the appropriate steps in this matter and, although he did not receive a complete approval at first, the breve of Innocent XI was already, in a sense, a recognition of Father Papczyński's work.

Not only Father Stanislaus alone but also his powerful protector, Bishop Wierzbowski, rejoiced in it. The Bishop even issued a special letter on this occasion dated May 22, 1681. In this letter he expressed a conviction that the Pope's breve constituted an indirect approval of the Congregation. Being certain now that his decision to erect Father Papczyński's institute in his diocese was right, he took the Marians under his protection once again, bestowed further privileges upon them, and expressed the wish that they would quickly grow and flourish in number and in merits.

He would later watch over the Congregation and remove all the obstacles threatening its development. However, difficulties kept arising and they would often come from the very members of the Marian community.

When a dispute between Father Stanislaus and his subordinates arose in 1685, Bishop Wierzbowski decided to intervene personally. He ordered a Warsaw official, Nicholas Stanislaus Święcicki, to appoint commissioners to investigate the matter. The commissioners acquainted themselves with the situation at the Cenacle and on June 11, 1685, gave dispositions aimed at healing the matter.

To restore peace and harmony at the monastery, they reaffirmed Father Papczyński's authority as the Superior and confirmed the validity of the requirements that he had set in matters of religious observance. On November 19, 1685, Bishop Wierzbowski re-confirmed the erection of the Congregation from 1679 and explained that Father Stanislaus was to be the Superior of both the Congregation and the Cenacle for life. Furthermore, he once again set the borders of the estate adjacent to the Cenacle. This was to stave off the frequent quarrels between the Marians and the inhabitants of New Jerusalem.

20. A SECOND ERECTION OF THE CONGREGATION

Bishop Wierzbowski's declaration from November 1685, could not fully protect Father Stanislaus's community from the attacks of its enemies. They would still use certain ambiguities and inaccuracies in the documents and ay claims to the Marians' properties. The never ending quarrels before various courts and other internal difficulties prompted Bishop Wierzbowski to perform a second erection of the Congregation of Marians.

In his document of February 21, 1687, he recalls how the Congregation of Marians was founded, how they established their house at the Cenacle, and how they were erected canonically in 1679. The purpose of the second erection was, primarily, to secure the Marians' rights of ownership in New Jerusalem. The Bishop solemnly reminded everyone that Father Papczyński and his Congregation were the only rightful and perpetual owners of the Cenacle and of all movables and immovables attached to the estate entrusted to their care.

To remove any remaining doubts, the Bishop once again set the borders of this estate. Finally, he made an appeal to the inhabitants of the town asking them not to attack the Congregation any longer and not to disturb its peace, but to support it in every possible way. He also appealed to his successors to keep the Marians in their care and to defend them.

The shepherd of Poznań drew up the act of the second erection of the Marians just two weeks before his death. At that time, he was already seriously ill and wanted very much to settle the matters regarding the Congregation of the Marians; the matters that were so close to his heart. Thus the erection document can be considered to be the last will left by the holy Bishop to his beloved Congregation of the Immaculate Conception. His personal testament bears the same date as the document in which the ailing Bishop announced the second erection of the Congregation. Simplicity and sincerity, great humility deep faith, and the love of God emanate from the pages of his testament.

Father Stanislaus often visited his dying protector and friend. Bishop Wierzbowski was worried that he could no leave much to the community in his last will. When Fathe Stanislaus asked him for a blessing during one of the las visits, the arch-prelate said that he was leaving the Marians Divine Providence in his last will. The Servant of God received this gift with great gratitude. From thi moment dates the devotion of the Marians to God' Providence. This devotion is expressed in the title of the Polish Province as well as in the annual feast at the Church of the Last Supper in Góra Kalwaria, which is cel ebrated to this day.

In the evening of March 6 or 7, 1687, Bishop Stepha Wierzbowski gave up his spirit to God. Bidding him a sor rowful farewell were not only the clergy and the faithfu but, first of all, Father Papczyński and his Congregatior Father Papczyński did not remain all alone after the deat of his protector. The following year Bishop Wierzbowski' relatives came to Góra (Kalwaria) and in the statemer dated October 26, 1688, confirmed the Marian foundatio and took the Congregation under their protection.

21. BESET BY NEW THREATS

Just as during his lifetime, similarly after the death of the founder of New Jerusalem, many groups of pilgrim were arriving at this sanctuary. The faithful visited the chapels, followed the paths of the Way of the Cross, pondering the mysteries of the Lord's Passion. Quite often Father Stanislaus would lead such a group, preach sermons in his church, in other local churches, or simply outside in the open. His solid theological preparation, deep spiritual life, and pedagogical talents bore beautiful fruit in the confessional. People of various social standing would come to him, bearing the burden of sins, doubts, or scruples. They left reconciled with God and with their spirits lifted.

Still, the development of his Congregation was the most important matter for the founder of the Marians. Father Stanislaus continued to improve his constitutions and, when they were finished, decided to have them published. He managed to obtain Bishop Wierzbowski's approval before he died, and published his "Rule of Life" in Warsaw in 1687.

In the constitutions approved by the Bishop of Poznań, the members of Father Papczyński's community were still referred to as "Clerics Recollect of the Most Blessed Virgin Mary Conceived without Sin," although the name "Marians" appeared as well. It was still a Congregation of an eremitical character whose members lived a very hard, almost penitential life. The duty of self-flagellation, keeping prayerful vigils at night, and observing strict fasts still existed. It would seem that such discipline should ensure the strength and stabilization of the Congregation.

However, the community was constantly exposed to the attacks of the enemies. The latter were often members of other religious communities. They regarded the Marians as their competitors more and more often sought out the courts of the nobility and tried to deprive the Marians of their privileges. They claimed that the Marians as "hermits" did not have the right to engage in apostolic work and they should not leave the walls of their monasteries.

After Bishop Wierzbowski's death, the greatest threat came from the least expected side, that is, his successor Bishop John Stanislaus Witwicki (1687-1696) took over the diocese of Poznań. The enemies of the Marians began to accuse them before the arch-prelate, again demanding the liquidation of the Congregation.

At first the Bishop seemed to lend his ear to their calumnies. Father Stanislaus knew exactly what it meant. Both his monasteries were located on the territory administered by Bishop Witwicki and were totally dependent on his will. The new Ordinary could withdraw his predecessor's approval, and the Congregation, which did not yet have the approbation of the Holy See, could be disbanded. This is just what Father Papczyński's enemies counted on.

Father Papczyński responded to the attacks of his adversaries in a truly Christian manner. He did not defend himself, did not try to explain, but, instead, dedicated to Bishop Witwicki the fruit of his meditations at the foot of Christ's cross — a book titled "Christus patiens" (*The Suffering Christ*), published in 1690 in Warsaw.

The booklet was a triumph of the Servant of God over those who wanted to harm him. He mentioned his enemies in his dedicatory letter to the bishop and asked for his protection. He expressed hope that nothing wrong would happen to him in the darkness of the night because the star shining in the bishop's coat of arms would disperse it. He could, therefore, remain at peace, just like the moon also visible in the bishop's coat of arms, and be unafraid of the barking pack of dogs attacking him.

The bishop, won over by this dedication and by the profundity of Father Stanislaus's meditations, became more critical of the accusations against Father Papczyński's Congregation. Having investigated the whole matter more carefully and without prejudice, he came to the conclusion that all the charges were unfounded.

22. FURTHER ATTEMPTS TO OBTAIN THE APPROBATION OF THE HOLY SEE

Once again Father Stanislaus' work was saved. But this was a great warning for him, and he realized how important it was to find better protection, in case something similar should happen in the future. It became absolutely necessary to obtain papal approbation so as not to be subordinate to the Bishop Ordinary's will.

Father Papczyński was going to make efforts to secure such an approbation for one other reason, namely, to obtain for the Marians the right to take solemn vows. He hoped that this might stop the ever more frequent departures from the Congregation because simple vows did not have, at least in the opinion of some moral theologians, as strong a binding power as solemn vows.

Since Father Stanislaus wanted to obtain the papal approbation as soon as possible, in 1690, he began to prepare himself to travel to the Eternal City. He wanted to attend to the matter personally, even though it would require making a long and dangerous journey, mostly on foot, because of the lack of funds. He did not know how this journey would end so, before he left, on October 30 1690, in the town of Czersk, he made a will in which he bequeathed the estate at the Cenacle to the members of his Congregation.

Accompanied by a subdeacon, Joachim of St. Anne Kozłowski, the Servant of God set out to Rome on a journey that was strenuous for him and full of surprises During this time he was often taken ill. He was almost 60 and, as we know, he lived a penitential life, so his strength often failed him. Joachim Kozłowski, who witnessed the hardships of this journey, would play an important role in the Congregation some time later. The young subdeacon brought Father Stanislaus to Rome in February of 1691 The Italian sky greeted them in mourning as Pope Alexander VIII died on February 1, and the See of Peter was orphaned.

One can imagine what a disappointment it was for Father Papczyński. The Servant of God did not give up and, after a confession with a papal confessor, Father Thomas Ignatius Dunin Szpot, SJ, in St. Peter's Basilica he decided to investigate the possibility of settling the matter that brought him to this city. It was not possible to obtain the papal approbation on the basis of "The Rule of Life," therefore, Father Stanislaus took the steps necessary to have his Congregation incorporated into the Order of the Sisters of the Immaculate Conception of the Blessed Virgin Mary. Since this order was subordinate to the Order of Franciscan Friars Minor, Father Papczyński submitted an appropriate petition to them in March or April of 1691, in which he asked the friars to take the Marians under their jurisdiction and to give them such privileges as those already enjoyed by the Sisters of the Immaculate Conception.

In answer to this request, the Superior General of the Friars Minor drew up a document on April 20, 1691, in which he took the Marians under his protection and commended them to the care of the superiors of his Order, especially in the Kingdom of Poland and the Grand Duchy of Lithuania. Later, the General Congregation of the Friars Minor confirmed the document drawn up by the Superior General, making the choice of the rule contingent upon the approval of the Holy See. It also accepted Father Stanislaus' request to take the Marians under the direction and jurisdiction of the Friars Minor. In the meantime, however, it was necessary to wait for the election of the new Pope.

Although the conclave started on February 12, 1691, it was becoming interminable. The waiting was getting more difficult for Father Stanislaus. He did find humble lodgings at the Friars Minor monastery in Aracoeli, but the approaching summer heat made his poor health deteriorate. The doctors advised a change of climate and a return to Poland. It was difficult to wait longer for the election of the Pope, then to obtain an audience, perhaps even after the summer, and risk a journey home during the winter. Therefore, the Servant of God decided to return to Poland in July.

Before he left Rome, he addressed a request to Father

Aleksy, the Superior General of the Piarists, to incorporate the Marians into their Congregation. The answer, which he received on May 27, 1691, demonstrates that the old animosity of the Piarists towards Father Stanislaus had disappeared. Moreover, their answer is a beautiful defense of the Servant of God and a splendid testimony of the help and benevolence which he had shown to the Piarists in Poland. The Piarists gladly allowed Father Stanislaus and his Congregation to share in the privileges bestowed upon them by the Holy See, especially to receive graces.

When the new Pope, Innocent XII, was finally elected on July 12, 1691, Father Stanislaus was no longer in Rome. He had left the Eternal City most likely on July 10 or 11, just before the election. It is supposed that just before his return to Poland, he had left his "Rule of Life" in the Congregation for Bishops and Religious, because he received its revised version in 1694, and there is no information in the documents that he sent it to Rome later.

After his return to Poland, the Servant of God — probably in the spring of 1692 — sent a petition to the Holy See, in which he presented the matters which he had wanted to discuss with the Pope personally. After considering the petition, on June 20, 1692, the Congregation sent it back to the Nuncio in Poland asking for an explanation. In the meantime, Father Papczyński sent a second petition to Rome in which he repeated his request for the approbation of his Congregation and its incorporation into the Order of the Sisters of the Immaculate Conception of the Blessed Virgin Mary, under the jurisdiction of the Superior General of the Friars Minor.

The Sacred Congregation ordered Father Papczyński to take the matter to the Pope himself. Soon Father Papczyński sent a request directly to Innocent XII and on September 5, 1692, a special committee of the Congregation considered it and sent it to the Nuncio in Poland. Meanwhile, on September 13, the petition of the founder of the Marians was presented to the Holy Father himself who ordered the Sacred Congregation to handle the matter. But the Congregation was waiting for the opinion of the Nuncio in Poland. He investigated the matter for almost a year, and in 1693, sent it back to Rome. During this time, Father Stanislaus became gravely ill and on December 9, 1692, he even prepared his last will.

Time was passing and it was only in 1694 that Father Papczyński's "Rule of Life" was sent back to Poland amended by Cardinal Leonard Colloredo. This answer did not make Father Papczyński happy, because it still did not grant his Congregation the approbation of the Holy See, and he had to remain content with the approval of the Bishop and the revised "Rule of Life." Later Father Stanislaus prepared it for publication and obtained the diocesan approval for it.

The only achievement of Father Stanislaus's prolonged efforts in Rome was an authoritative statement by the Sacred Congregation that the Bishop Ordinary's approval was sufficient for the Marians. Father Papczyński refers to this statement in Praefatio Informatoria (Preface) to "The Rule of Life" and argues that, contrary to the claims of the Marians' enemies, his Congregation does not need the approbation of the Holy See to be able to exist as a legal entity. However, this does not satisfy him. Soon he makes another attempt at obtaining the approbation of the Holy See for his Congregation.

23. THE APPROBATION OF THE CONGREGATION BY THE HOLY SEE

On March 4, 1698, Bishop Witwicki died and Hieronim Wierzbowski, a relative of the late Bishop Stephen Wierzbowski, became his successor in the diocese of Poznań. Now Father Papczyński could again count on the Bishop Ordinary's support for his efforts because as we know, the Wierzbowski family had promised such support in 1688. Soon the founder of the Marians needed it very much.

At a general chapter convened by Father Papczyński in the summer of 1698, Father Joachim of St. Anne Kozłowski was elected Procurator General and sent to Rome to resume the efforts to obtain papal approbation. In the fall of 1698 Father Kozłowski left accompanied by Brother Anthony Cieński and supplied with a letter of recommendation from Bishop Hieronim Wierzbowski.

After they had arrived in Rome, Father Joachim obtained an audience with Pope Innocent XII and submitted to him the petition regarding approbation of the Congregation of Marians. The Pope knew Father Papczyński very well, at some point he was his penitent when he was staying in Warsaw as the Apostolic Nuncio. Out of kindness for his former confessor he intended, at first, to approve the Congregation of the Marians and their

"Rule of Life." But the cardinals, whose advice he asked, dissuaded him from doing so, referring to the decree issued by the Council in Lateran in 1215, forbidding the approval of religious institutes with rules other than those that had already been approved.

Father Kozłowski was not discouraged by the negative answer and continued his efforts. In January of 1699, he wrote a letter to Father Papczyński asking him to seek the support for his efforts in Rome from highly placed persons, both clerical and lay, in Poland.

Father Stanislaus managed to obtain letters of recommendation as well. Father Kozłowski received them in May. One of the letters, written by Bishop Hieronim Wierzbowski and dated March 20, 1699, is a beautiful testimony to the virtues of Father Stanislaus and his companions in the Congregation.

After Father Kozłowski had received the letters of recommendation, he submitted another petition to the offices of the Holy See requesting approval of the Congregation, but, again, he did not obtain apostolic approbation on the basis of "The Rule of Life."

Since it was impossible to receive papal approbation for the Congregation through adoption of "The Rule of Life," the Procurator General of the Marians began to look for another solution. There was a possibility of obtaining approbation on the basis of a rule that had already been approved. Father Bonaventure Diaz, OFM, advised Father Kozłowski to adopt the Rule of the Ten Virtues of the Blessed Virgin Mary written by the Blessed Gabriel Maria for the Sisters of the Annunciation. It was approved in 1502 by Pope

Alexander VI. Later, in 1517, the orders adopting this rule were put under the jurisdiction of the Friars Minor.

Following Father Bonaventure's advice, Father Joachim turned to Father Matthew of St. Stephen, the Superior General of the Friars Minor, asking him to incorporate the Marians into his Order. Father Matthew agreed and, on September 21, 1699, in the Aracoeli monastery, drew up the document expected by the Marian envoys. It was now necessary to obtain "de facto" all the privileges, graces, and indulgences attached to this rule.

To this end, Father Joachim sent a request to Pope Innocent XII, probably in October of 1699. In return he received a breve titled "Exponi nobis super" and dated November 24, 1699. The breve was, in fact, a letter to the Apostolic Nuncio in Poland informing him that the Marians had adopted the "Rule of Ten Virtues" in brotherly communion with the Franciscan Order. The letter mentioned that the Marians had obtained the privileges and graces granted to all religious institutes which had adopted the same rule. The Pope threatened to punish those who would question the rights given to the Marians and obligated the Apostolic Nuncio to make sure that the orders contained in the letter mentioned above were carried out.

It is not known why, after receiving such a valuable document, Father Joachim remained in Rome for another year. There must have been some reasons which made him postpone his return home. He was to leave Rome after September 18, 1700, as can be inferred from the last letter of recommendation which he obtained for his Congregation in Rome. But even this later date of his departure was put off, perhaps in anticipation of Pope Innocent XII's approaching death. It was wise to wait for the election of the new Pope and obtain from him a confirmation of his predecessor's breve.

Soon, indeed, on September 27, 1700, Pope Innocent XII passed away, and on November 23, his successor, Clement XI, was elected. He confirmed the document issued by his predecessor and sent an order to Francis Pignatelli, the Apostolic Nuncio in Poland, to receive the solemn profession from Father Stanislaus Papczyński, the founder of the Marians.

Now nothing else was keeping Father Joachim and his companion, Brother Cieński, in the Eternal City. So they set out on their journey back to Poland, carrying with them the papal documents along with the letters of recommendation from the cardinals of the Roman Curia to the Apostolic Nuncio and the Primate of Poland.

24. A NEW MARIAN HOUSE

While the Procurator General of the Marians was still in Rome, the Congregation received a new, third foundation. John Lasocki of Glew founded a church and a monastery for the Marians in Goźlin, on the territory of the parish of Wilga. The erection document was drawn up in Czersk on October 15, 1699, but the necessary formalities had already begun in 1698, when, on September 11, the church authorities gave permission to build a chapel in Goźlin and install the Marians there. The formal installation took place eight days after the act of donation was drawn up in the town of Czersk.

Soon, in 1700, the construction of the church was finished. According to tradition, a picture of Our Sorrowful Lady, which Father Papczyński had brought from his family home in Podegrodzie, was placed in the church. Perhaps the founder of the Marians brought the picture in the summer of 1699, when he went on a pilgrimage to the Diocese of Cracow.

Did the Marians have any other houses during the lifetime of their founder? Probably so, perhaps one in Russia and one in Lithuania, but, at present, there are no documents to confirm it.

25. THE SOLEMN PROFESSION OF THE FIRST MARIANS

Waiting for the return of the bearers of good news who had been sent to Rome was a very difficult time for Father Stanislaus. He was already advanced in years and seriously ill, and his envoys were late in returning. Finally, probably towards the end of March 1701, they arrived in New Jerusalem. One can imagine the joy of the ailing founder when the bearers of the grace of the Holy See appeared at the gates of his monastery. The work of his life was successfully concluded and he could now prepare himself to leave this world.

Father Stanislaus' joy was somewhat dimmed when he read the documents brought from Rome. The constitutions which he had prepared were not approved. Instead he had to accept a new rule and the fact that his Congregation was incorporated into the Order of the Friars Minor.

Later, however, he became convinced that "The Rule of the Ten Virtues" was not contradictory to the statutes which he had prepared for his Congregation and that it corresponded with the spirit of his own intentions. It did, after all, fervently encourage the imitation of the virtues of the Blessed Virgin Conceived without Sin, and it was the Marians, first of all, who should practice these virtues. Nevertheless Father Papczyński reproached Father Kozłowski for failing to obtain the approval of "The Rule of Life" as the Marian constitutions now had to adapt to the "Rule of the Ten Virtues" mentioned earlier.

When Francis Pignatelli, the Apostolic Nuncio, received the letter of Innocent XII and the order of Clement XI regarding the solemn profession of Father Papczyński and his spiritual sons, he demanded from them a written consent that they would make their solemn vows on the "Rule of the Ten Virtues." Father Papczyński and the representatives of all Marian houses expressed such a consent during the chapter on April 14, 1701 in New Jerusalem.

But it was only on June 6 that ailing Father Stanislaus was able to go to Warsaw and make his solemn profession before the Apostolic Nuncio. The Nuncio ordered the founder of the Marians to receive the solemn profession from other members of the Congregation. On July 5, 1701, Father Joseph of All Saints made his profession, followed by the other confreres. Thus, the Marians became an order under papal law and received the rights and privileges vested in all clerical orders with solemn vows.

The papal document of November 24, 1699 does not

refer to them as hermits or "recollects" any longer. Father Papczyński himself, who from the very beginning envisioned the Marians as an apostolic Congregation, calls his confreres "Clerici Mariani." At the time, the Marians were quite often referred to as a Congregation or institute helping the dead and the pastors in parishes.

26. THE LAST MONTHS OF
FATHER PAPCZYŃSKI'S LIFE

After making his solemn profession and receiving such profession from his confreres, Father Papczyński did not have much time left in his life on earth. The Servant of God began to prepare himself to die. Already, in 1695, as he felt that he was losing his strength, he delegated part of his authority to Father Kozłowski, who was elected his vicar by the provincial chapter. On April 16 of the same year, Father Papczyński called the members of the Congregation to be obedient to Father Kozłowski, in whom he saw his successor. He himself still fulfilled the duties of the Superior of the monastery in New Jerusalem.

But in 1699, crushed by his illness, he handed this function over to Father Cyprian of St. Stanislaus. In the same year he made his second will, and declared Father Joachim to be his successor. He confirmed and amended this will on April 10, 1701, when a new grave illness forced him to take to his bed. He rose from it to go to Warsaw to make his solemn profession before the Apostolic Nuncio. The "Praecepta" (Admonitions), which come from this period of his life, indicate that he probably made the last canonical visitation of the Korabiew Forest at that time.

In August, he was afflicted by another serious illness which proved to be fatal. Father Stanislaus made another addition to his will and gave his last dispositions. Meanwhile, the illness violently ravaged his body and the sufferings grew more acute. Consumed by fever, he was coherent and lucid till the very end. On September 17, 1701, fully conscious, he received the Holy Sacraments (Viaticum) from Father Joseph of All Saints, the first priest ordained in the Congregation. Afterwards he gave his last blessing to the confreres surrounding his bed and urged them to persevere in the faithful observance of the rule and the constitutions, and to be particularly zealous in helping the souls suffering in Purgatory.

As he drew his last breath, he was grasping the crucifix and praying fervently. The last words that could be heard coming from his lips were: "Into Your hands, Lord, I commend my spirit." He fell asleep in the Lord on September 17, 1701, in the evening, as the sun faded and disappeared below the horizon.

The funeral of the founder of the Marians drew great crowds of priests, religious, and the faithful mourning his death. They all testified to Father Stanislaus' holiness and commended themselves to his intercession. He was buried reverently under the floor of the Church of the Last Supper, near the altar of St. Raphael.

27. A SPIRITUAL PORTRAIT OF THE SERVANT OF GOD

Every impartial researcher into Father Stanislaus Papczyński's life and activity must admit that he was an extraordinary man. His life, pastoral work, his work as a founder of a religious order, and his literary output testify to the fact that he was a man of great caliber. This picture is completed by his equally rich spiritual portrait.

His biographers point out that it was quite early, when he still lived with his family, that he began to make great progress in acquiring virtues, and, during his studies, he distinguished himself by great humility and other spiritual attributes. When he was in the Piarist novitiate, he was known for his great zeal in the spiritual life, and in practicing the virtues. Later, too, he was referred to as a model of exemplary religious life and Christian perfection.

After he had left the Piarists, during the period preceding the founding of the Congregation of Marians, many of his contemporaries, among whom were often eminent personages, considered him to be a man of great sanctity. When he lived in the Korabiew Forest, news about his piety and holiness spread very quickly. In New Jerusalem, according to the testimony of his contemporaries, Father Papczyński lived a saintly life during his entire stay there, till the day he died, setting an example of heroism in practicing virtues.

Among the virtues which the life of Servant of God exemplified, his faith, love, humility, and courage merit our special attention. From his very early youth, Father

Papczyński distinguished himself by the spirit of deep faith and piety. He expressed this faith and piety by building little altars, participating in the religious devotions in his parish church, and turning with earnest trust to God and the Most Holy Virgin in various difficulties and dangers. While still a novice, he was not afraid to die for the holy faith when he was attacked by a Swedish soldier on the street in Warsaw. It was his faith that helped him to bear many persecutions, when he was at the Piarists, and to overcome the great difficulties connected with the founding of a new religious family. His deep faith was the source of his trust and absolute reliance on Divine Providence.

From his childhood, Father Papczyński had remained in deep communion with God and managed to establish intimate ties with Him. He was always guided by the love of God and neighbor. He practiced such love zealously all his life. He always hastened to people with great love, to serve them in the confessional, from the pulpit, and in personal contacts; he always showed great compassion for the poor and orphaned. He was always patient, although sometimes strict, in admonishing his confreres, and he was magnanimous in forgiving his enemies and persecutors. Christian love prompted him to come to the aid of the souls suffering in Purgatory.

Many of Father Stanislaus's contemporaries considered him to be a man of great humility. In the novitiate, he joyfully performed the lowest tasks. He did not try to find excuses for his conduct or to explain his "faults" to the superiors questioning him at one of the chapters, but bore the false accusations with courage. After leaving the

Piarists, he rejected the honors and offices which the bishops were offering to him. As the founder of the Marians, he personally did a lot of hard physical work, especially in the early stages. His contemporaries testified that he was quite unusual in humiliating himself, and that he rejoiced when others spoke badly of him.

He dedicated himself totally to the matters of God, as they were always most important to him. He proved it during the Swedish invasion when he was ready to give up his life for the holy faith. As he himself claimed, God spared him then for longer suffering. He experienced it soon during the persecutions at the Piarists. He bore it all with great patience, steadfastness, and serenity. He accepted the persecutions and animosity from the incipient religious community with great courage. With the same courage he bore many illnesses and sufferings as he prepared himself to leave this world.

Sketching the spiritual portrait of Father Papczyński, one cannot forget about his spirit of penance and mortification. This spirit was already evident in his early youth. When he entered the Piarists, his superiors noticed immediately that he was very moderate in taking food and drink, resistant to cold weather, and willing to perform the most difficult chores. He accepted all discomforts and persecutions in the spirit of penance. With the same disposition he accepted his imprisonment by the Piarists and the humiliation connected with it. Later on he gladly accepted Bishop Święcicki's severe decrees and lived, according to his orders, the life of a hermit in the Korabiew Forest.

He kept strict fasts, often scourged himself, spent his

nights in prayer, and when he lay down to rest, he was content with a simple bedding. He also performed hard physical labor and made long apostolic journeys on foot. During his stay at New Jerusalem, he continued his penitential life. Father Papczyński paid even greater attention to spiritual mortification which was a special quality of his spirituality. "The Rule of Life" which he wrote orders the restraint of one's feelings, desires, judgement, and will. In many letters to the members of the Congregation, he reminded them about the need for constant mortification, diligence, and sobriety.

It goes without saying that a man of such a deep spirituality possessed other virtues at the level of heroism. His life provides a great deal of evidence that he practiced the virtue of hope and recommended it to others. It was hope that made him rely on God's goodness and Providence even in the most difficult moments of his life. The Servant of God distinguished himself by the virtues of discernment and justice throughout his entire adult life. He was untiring in prayer, particularly for the souls suffering in Purgatory.

As a religious and founder of a new order, he valued very highly living the message of the Gospel. His service to God and people, in chastity, poverty and obedience, was combined with a fervent devotion to the Immaculately Conceived Blessed Virgin. No wonder that God supported the life of such a faithful servant with many signs such as: visions and revelations, the gift of prophecy and spiritual discernment, and the gift of performing miracles.

28. SPECIAL GRACES IN THE LIFE OF
THE FOUNDER OF THE MARIANS

Father Papczyński's first biographer, Leporini, recalls that in November of 1673 the Servant of God saw in ecstasy the victory of the Polish army over the Turks at Chocim. Another fact deserving our special attention is the vision of St. Joseph Calasantius during which he was admonished with regard to the steps that he should be taking as a founder of a new religious order.

His second biographer, Father Casimir Wyszyński, wrote that one day, probably some time in 1675, during his prayer for the soldiers fallen in battle against the Turkish onslaught, many souls suffering in Purgatory appeared to Father Stanislaus begging him to never stop coming to their aid. Both biographers recorded an event when the Servant of God, sitting at the table among many guests in the house of the Karski family, experienced an ecstasy in which he was present in Purgatory where he watched the immense suffering of innumerable souls. He had many such visions.

One of Father Stanislaus' contemporaries, Sister Ottilia, a Dominican nun, testified that he was commonly referred to as a prophet. According to the testimony of the witnesses living in the 18th century, the Servant of God, enlightened by the spirit of prophecy, foretold many things from the future. Leporini confirms that Father Papczyński, endowed with the grace of spiritual discernment, helped many penitents of timid conscience in regaining peace and dispersing doubts.

The witnesses in the information process testified that

Father Papczyński had a gift of performing miracles. One day, by making the sign of the cross, he dispersed a cloud threatening the faithful who were listening to his sermon that he was giving outdoors. The Servant of God possessed, too, the grace of healing the sick, especially children. With his earnest prayer he obtained the healing of the Karski's son who had been gravely ill.

According to the testimony of Mr. Magnuszewski, a witness in the information process, and to tradition as well, Father Papczyński even possessed the gift of raising the dead.

Father Papczyński's power to obtain miracles has survived to our times.

29. THE POSTHUMOUS CULT OF THE SERVANT OF GOD

The first Marians showed great reverence for the bodily remains of their founder, which bespeaks their conviction of his sanctity.

During the funeral, the coffin with Father Stanislaus' body was buried with due reverence in a shallow grave dug in wet ground under the floor of the church. The walls of the grave were covered with logs and three fitted beams closed it from the top.

Father Papczyński's grave was opened for the first time in 1705, four years after his death. It was discovered that his body remained quite undamaged, only his face around the nose was somewhat decayed. His habit was not damaged, either, although the coffin rotted through in the wet soil.

The grave was reopened during Bishop Adam Rostkowski's canonical visitation of the Cenacle in either 1716 or 1721. It was discovered again that the body was not damaged. It did begin to decay only within the next several years when water flooded the monastery grounds and the floor of the church. The rotten beams crushed the coffin and pressed the body of the Servant of God into the mud, so that after some time only his bones remained.

Father Casimir Wyszyński, who had been Superior General of the Congregation since 1737, exhumed them in 1740 with the Bishop's permission. He removed the bones from the mud and put them in a different coffin. Then, in 1752, Father Kajetan Wetycki, the Superior General of the Congregation, made a new coffin.

Father Papczyński's coffin was opened for the last time in 1766, with the permission of Felix Turski, the Bishop of Chełm and, at the same time, Bishop Auxiliary of Warsaw. At that time, due to the efforts of the Superior General, Father Hyacinth Wasilewski, a sarcophagus was built near the main altar and the coffin with the remains of the Servant of God was placed inside without any inscription. To this day this sarcophagus is in the Church of the Last Supper in Góra Kalwaria. Towards the end of the 19th century a plaque was placed on the sarcophagus, with the following inscription:

IN MEMORY OF
STANISLAUS PAPCZYŃSKI
FOUNDER OF THE CONGREGATION
OF THE MARIAN FATHERS
DIED IN THE YEAR 1701, ON SEPTEMBER 17
HE LIVED 70 YEARS

Immediately after the death of the founder of the Marians, veneration to him began to spread, not only in New Jerusalem and the area, but also in Lithuania and Podolia. The Marians brought it also to Portugal and Rome. Below are a few testimonies of the people who knew Father Papczyński personally and were deeply convinced of his sanctity.

Ottilia, a Dominican nun, convinced of Father Stanislaus' sanctity, testified around the year 1760, that he was a holy man. Martin Świdziński, who was healed in 1698 through Father Papczyński's intercession, preserved till the year 1774, when he gave this testimony, an unfading memory of his piety. Father G. Wolski, OFM, who met Father Papczyński in 1698, said about him in 1725, that he was already in heaven with all the saints, and he commended himself to his prayers.

In the 18th century, numerous healings occurred through the intercession of the Servant of God, Father Papczyński. In 1754, Nicholas Twarowski's dying daughter was healed after invoking Father Papczyński's help. In the same year two Portuguese men, who had been very seriously ill, regained their health through his intercession. Around the year 1766, Simon Krasuski of Skórzec, ill in bed for a few weeks, and without any hope of getting better, regained his health after he had invoked Father Papczyński's help. In 1767, Teophila Morawska, suffering severely from the complications of childbirth, and abandoned by her doctors, regained her health through Father Stanislaus' intercession. In 1771, Andrew Kuszewski's son, tormented by convulsions for twelve days and nights, was healed through the intercession of the Servant of God.

During the years 1752 to 1769, the Marians gathered many testimonies confirming the opinion of Father Stanislaus' sanctity. These testimonies were given by people who had either been healed through Father Stanislaus' intercession or had received other graces. In the years 1750 to 1752, the belief in his sanctity was strongly held by the Piarists in Lithuania. Father Wyszyński reported that the Piarists in Rome also venerated Father Papczyński around 1752.

In 1752, Adam I. Komorowski, the Archbishop of Gniezno and the Primate of Poland, wrote to Joseph Emmanuel I, the King of Portugal, that the memory of the Servant of God was still alive in Poland. His memory was also alive in Portugal, especially in Lisbon, where many people were obtaining graces through Father Papczyński's intercession. In 1757, a translation of his biography was published there, pictures of him became available, and a statue of him was erected. Father Wyszyński reported that in Rome, too, Father Papczyński was venerated by many of the faithful.

It is worth mentioning that the Marians did not say the Office for the Dead or celebrate Mass for the soul of their Founder on the anniversary of his death because they were convinced that he did not need such help. They would sing "Te Deum" instead.

In 1748, printed images of Father Papczyński appeared with an inscription "Ven. Dei Servus." The opinion of his sanctity was corroborated in each of the three biographies written about him in the form of an eulogy in the 18th century. The first one was written in Poland, around 1705, by Mansueto Leporini, OFM Ref., who was the Marians' Novice Master at that time. In 1754, Father Wyszyński wrote the second, more extensive one at the request of the Portuguese. The third biography, which was, in fact, a free translation of the previous one, done by Father Joao Teixeir, was published in Portugal in 1757.

30. THE PATH TO BEATIFICATION

The matter of Father Stanislaus Papczyński's elevation to the honors of the altar became of great concern to Father Wyszyński. He was convinced that God's blessing for the community was contingent upon the efforts made to obtain the beatification of their founder. He experienced this blessing when he took care of Father Stanislaus' grave. He maintained that, after the remains of the Servant of God had been exhumed, he felt clearly blessed. Later, when he was in Rome, he urged the superiors in Poland to start preparations leading to the opening of the beatification process. It pained him greatly that the matter was getting delayed and, in the meantime, the number of the living witnesses who could give testimony about the life and virtues of the founder of the Marians was growing smaller.

Indeed, the matter of Father Papczyński's beatification was still remote, and it was only half a century after his death that some concrete steps were taken in this regard. There were various reasons for this delay, among others, the lack of knowledge of proper procedures and the lack of direct contacts with Rome.

As soon as the conditions became favorable, the Marians began the efforts towards the beatification of their founder. Between 1751 and 1753, Father Wyszyński made the first steps regarding this matter in Rome and sent instructions necessary to begin the information process. Between 1752 and 1757, Kajetan Wetycki, the Superior General of the Congregation, ordered the Marians to begin gathering the testimonies to the sanctity of life of the Servant of God and to the miracles obtained through his intercession. In 1753, the same Superior General ordered that the prayers for beatification should be said in all Marian monasteries.

Within a short time, multitudes of the Polish people, among them many bishops, princes, and magnates, sent petitions to Rome asking for the beatification of the Servant of God. The Polish Parliament also supported the cause with its decree from 1764. Finally, at the request of the Marians' General Chapter of August 24, 1766, the Bishop's Court, acting on behalf of the Bishop Ordinary of Poznań, began on June 10, 1767, the long-awaited information process. It lasted till October 4, 1769. The documents from the process, confirmed by the Bishop Ordinary of Poznań Andrew Stanislaus Młodziejowski, were sent to Rome.

The beatification process that had started so successfully was interrupted in 1775 due to incompetence in gathering the evidence. The political calamities which affected Poland towards the end of the 18th century made the contacts with the Holy See more difficult and frustrated efforts to resume the beatification process.

Although the beatification process of the Servant of God

was interrupted, the belief in his virtues never weakened, and the Marians tried very hard to resume the process.

In the 19th century, many publications praising Father Papczyński's greatness and virtues became available. In 1891, Father Pielasiński obtained permission to consecrate the Church of the Last Supper, which was practically raised from its ruins, and in which Father Stanislaus' remains were buried.

The 20th century brings a rich bibliography about the Servant of God. Many authors present in their articles a proposal to resume Father Papczyński's beatification process. They inform us about pilgrimages to his tomb and graces obtained through his intercession. In 1964, a historical committee gathered 353 letters from different parts of Poland, written between 1932 and 1962. Their authors speak about various graces obtained through Father Stanislaus' intercession, such as: regaining health, having prayers answered, obtaining effective help in a difficult financial and spiritual situation. Some of the letters mentioned above contain accounts of events which may be classified as miracles in the strict sense of the word.

The Congregation of Marians, renovated in 1909 after it had been liquidated by the tsarist authorities, began preparations to continue the matter of Father Papczyński's beatification with a renewed zeal when Poland regained her independence. The necessary archival materials were gathered, various publications and essays became available, and many pilgrimages came to the tomb of the Servant of God. However, it was only after World War II, in 1952, that the General Council of the Congregation of

Marians appointed the Postulator, who took the cause of their founder's beatification into his hands.

After the necessary documents had been gathered and presented to the Sacred Congregation for the Saints, the Historical Section of the Congregation took over Father Papczyński's case. Monsignor P.A. Frutaz, the Relator of this section at the time, ordered the appointment of a Historical Committee to gather the documents confirming that the reknown of Father Papczyński's sanctity continued without interruption. Such a committee was appointed by the Ordinary of Warsaw, Cardinal S. Wyszyński. It made the necessary inquiries and confirmed that the reknown of Father Papczyński's sanctity indeed continued without interruption. On the basis of the documents gathered and investigated scientifically by the Committee, the Historical Section could begin to work on "Positio super introductione Causae."

The Historical Section appointed Father K. KrzyIanowski, MIC, to do this work. Working under the direction of the then Relator General, he prepared the "Position" mentioned above. However, when this work was finished, there were difficulties with publishing it. Cardinal Wyszyński's persistent appeals to Pope Paul VI brought about the relatively quick publication of the "Position."

The "Position" was first evaluated by historical consultants. They debated whether this work contained sufficient information about the life and work of the Servant of God, and whether it would be possible to make a judgement about his moral character on its basis. The majority of the consultants considered the "Position" to be sufficient to continue the work in the Sacred Congregation for the Saints.

Following the positive opinion of the consultants, the General Congregation also gave its approval. Meanwhile, the Holy Father received letters of recommendation from the Plenary Conference of the Polish Episcopate and from the Councils of Male and Female Religious Orders in Poland. On March 6, 1981, following the decision of the Holy Father, John Paul II, a decree of the Congregation for the Saints was issued announcing the introduction of Father Papczyński's cause before the Apostolic Tribunal.

The process to establish that the decrees of Pope Urban VIII regarding the cult of saints were observed took place in Warsaw from 1981 to 1982. Its conclusion was that the church regulations concerning the public veneration of Father Papczyński at his tomb had been followed.

Then, on the basis of the materials gathered in the "Position", it was necessary to prove the heroic quality of Father Stanislaus Papczyński's virtues, before the Congregation for Saints, according to a new procedure in force since 1983.

Finally, on June 13, 1992, the Holy See recognized the heroic virtues of the Servant of God Father Stanislaus, who now bears the title of "Venerable". Thus, a miracle obtained by his intercession and recognized as such by the Holy See, is now the only thing necessary for his beatification.

What does "Venerable Servant of God" mean? It means that after thoroughly examining all available evidence, the Church has found sufficient proof that the person in question had reached such a state of holiness that he or she acted consistently with perfect virtue.

AN EXCERPT FROM FATHER PAPCZYŃSKI'S LAST WILL & TESTAMENT:

I give thanks to God in His Majesty for all the graces, gifts, and goodness which He bestowed upon me with great generosity. I regret with all my heart and, out of my love for God, I want to regret even more, all my sins which I place in the dearest Wounds of Jesus Christ, my Lord and Redeemer. I fall to the feet of the Blessed Virgin Mary, the Mother of God, and to her I commend myself and our tiny Congregation of her Immaculate Conception for all eternity, asking her gracious guidance and efficacious care. At the hour of death, I beg her most merciful and most powerful protection from the ambushes of my enemies and from all temporal and eternal evil. To all those who loved and supported this Congregation of the Immaculate Conception which, with God's inspiration I founded to help the faithful departed, I promise a double reward from God's hands.

I eagerly suggest to my brethren and, if I may say so my sons, that they should have love for God and neighbor devotion to the Catholic faith, reverence, love and obedience to the Holy See, faithful perseverance in the vows humility and patience; that they should help the souls in Purgatory and be at peace with everyone.

31. PRAYER FOR THE BEATIFICATION

Most holy and undivided Trinity, You choose to live in the hearts of Your faithful servants, and after their death to reward their merits with the glory of heaven. Grant, we implore You, that Your Servant Stanislaus, who with apostolic zeal faithfully served the Church under the patronage of the Immaculate Virgin Mary, may be numbered among the Blessed, through Christ our Lord. Amen.

32. PRAYER FOR A SPECIAL GRACE

O God, Merciful Father, in the heart of Your Servant Stanislaus You aroused such a great zeal for accomplishing corporal and spiritual deeds of mercy; deign to grant me (to us) through his intercession the grace ... for which (we) implore You ... Amen.

Our Father ... Hail Mary ... Glory be to the Father

Note : It is recommended that this prayer, recited for a particular intention, be complemented by Confession and Holy Communion.

Information about graces received through the intercession of the Venerable Servant of God, Father Stanislaus Papczyński, and applications from those wishing to become priests or brothers – followers of Mary Immaculate in the service of Christ and the Church, in the Congregation of the Marians – should be sent to the following address:

Br. Andrew R. Mączyński, MIC
Vice-Postulator of the
Marian Causes of Canonization
Eden Hill
Stockbridge, MA 01263

This monument marks the birthplace of Father Founder in his native village of Podegrodzie in Poland.

The parish church in the Venerable Servant's home village of Podegrodzie, Poland, set against the backdrop of the surrounding countryside.

Miraculous image of Our Lady, which, according to tradition, was displayed in the room where Father Founder was born. The image was bequeathed to the Marian monastery at Goźlin, Poland, when it was founded in 1699. Shortly thereafter, people began to pray to Our Lady before the image in the monastery church and to report that they had received special graces.

Church in Brzozowo where the Venerable Servant of God was ordained a priest on March 12, 1661, by the Most Rev. Stanislaus Sarnowski, Bishop of Przemyśl. At that time, Fr. Stanislaus Papczyński was a member of the Piarist Order and was nearly 30 years old.

Dramatic depiction of Father Founder as a chaplain on the battlefield. It was painted by A. L. Maj in 1934 and is from the Marian monastery in Warsaw-Praga, Poland. The heavenly figure shown above is the Blessed Mother holding the Infant Jesus.

One of the oldest extant portraits painted of Father Founder, which is from the second half of the 18th Century. This portrait was painted by Marian Br. Francis Niemirowski (d. 1795). In his day, Br. Francis was a very talented painter whose works were much in demand. The painting is from the Marians' monastery in Mariampole, Lithuania.

This is the original document of the Venerable Servant of God's act of profession in the Piarist Order. The profession took place on July 22, 1656, at the Piarist novitiate in Warsaw, Poland. Father Founder was then 25 years old.

This depiction of Father Founder interceding for the souls in Purgatory shows how he was guided in his prayer for the deceased by Mary as the Immaculate Conception (notice the heavenly figure of Mary Immaculate above him).

This painting is from Góra Kalwaria, Father Founder's burial place, and was painted by an anonymous artist of the 18th Century.

This is the oldest extant portrait of Fr. Stanislaus Papczyński. It was painted by an anonymous artist around the turn of the 17th and 18th centuries and is housed in the Marian monastery in Skórzec. To this day nobody is certain of the meaning of the Latin letters in the painting placed above Father Founder's head. Scholars have proposed a few different sayings in Latin as possible solutions.

Bishop Stephen Wierzbowski was a friend and protector of Fr. Stanislaus Papczyński and of his order in its early days of existence. Bishop Wierzbowski gave approval to the erection of the order within his diocese of Poznań and encouraged Father Founder to seek the Holy See's approbation for his order. This portrait of the bishop was painted by an anonymous artist in the 17th Century.

One of the oldest portraits of the Venerable Servant of God from the first part of the 18th Century, from the birthplace of the Marians in Puszcza Mariańska.

An 18th Century brass engraving of the Venerable Savior of God by an anonymous artist.

Stone Sculpture of Father Founder in front of the little Church of the Cenacle in Góra Kalwaria, the site of the Venerable Servant of God's burial. This striking likeness of Fr. Stanislaus was sculpted by Andrew Koss in 1985.

The white sarcophagus which bears the earthly remains of Fr. Stanislaus Papczyński, the Founder of the Marians of the Immaculate Conception.